J
629.132 Behrens, June
BE
      I can be a pilot

$13.27

DATE			
JA 23 '91	JUN 21 '94	FEB 23 '99	
FE 8 '91	AUG 18 '99	JE 1 '99	AG 14 '02
MY 13 '91	NOV 17 '94	AG 07 '00	JE 30 '04
JY 19 '91	JAN 19 '95	NV 16 '00	MY 21 '05
AG 20 '91	MAY 08 '95	JY 02 '01	AG 01 '05
FE 13 '92	AUG 05 '98	JY 16 '01	AP 12 '07
AP 1 '92	NOV 23 '98	AG 13 '01	AG 11 '08
MY 19 '92	MAR 28 '97	NO 22 '01	AG 16 '08
NO 11 '92	FEB 12 '98	JY 12 '02	JY 16 '09
JE 29 '93	OCT 06 '98	AG 05 '02	DE 14 '09
		AG 12 '02	NO 7 '12

MY 25 '12
AG 7 1 '77

© THE BAKER & TAYLOR CO.

I CAN BE A

PILOT

By June Behrens

Prepared under the direction of Robert Hillerich, Ph.D.

The author wishes to acknowledge with thanks the assistance of Captain Paul Warf, United Airlines, Ret.

CHILDRENS PRESS ®

CHICAGO

Library of Congress Cataloging in Publication Data
Behrens, June.
  I can be a pilot.

  Includes index.
  Summary: Explains the training pilots go through
before they can fly various kinds of airplanes.
  1. Air pilots—Juvenile literature.
[1. Air pilots. 2. Occupations] I. Title.
TL547.B39   1985   629.132'52'023   85-10961
ISBN 0-516-01888-4

PICTURE DICTIONARY

cargo

helicopter

instruments

physical exam

captain   **copilot**

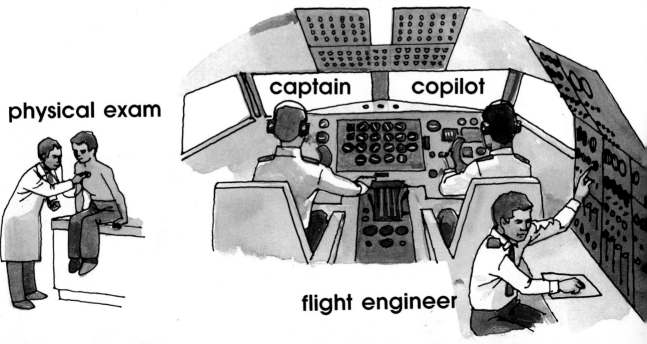

flight engineer

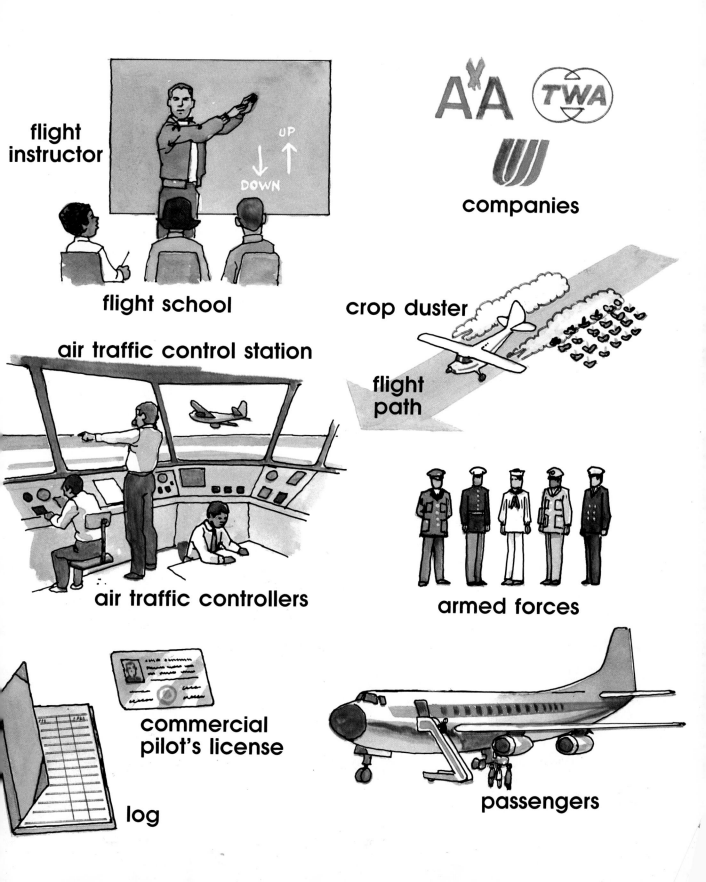

flight
instructor

flight school

companies

crop duster

flight
path

air traffic control station

air traffic controllers

armed forces

commercial
pilot's license

log

passengers

UP

DOWN

Big jets are flown by a pilot and a copilot (above). Only one pilot is needed to fly smaller planes (below).

The DC-10 has three jet engines.

Have you ever watched a big jet move across the sky? Have you ever wondered what it would be like to fly? Would you like to fly a plane?

The Concorde (above) is a supersonic jet. It can
fly 1,550 miles per hour. The propeller-driven
plane (below) can travel at less than 400 miles per hour.

Crew of Thai Airways International

People who fly airplanes or helicopters are called pilots. Pilots carry passengers and cargo. They may fly to the next city or go to faraway places.

helicopter

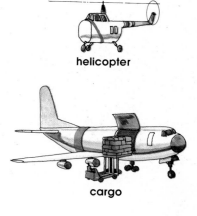

cargo

passengers

armed forces

commercial
pilot's license

Pilots learn to fly in flying schools. Some colleges have flying classes. Many pilots learned to fly in the armed forces. Pilots must work hard to earn their pilot's license.

Many pilots learned to fly when they served in the army, navy, marines, air force, or coast guard. Others go to flying schools.

Most students learn to fly propeller-driven planes.

Pilots must have a
commercial pilot's
license to fly. They must
be eighteen years old
with at least 250 hours of
flying time. They must
pass a written test and a
flying test.

Many pilots are
licensed to fly by using
instruments that tell them
where their airplane is.
For this license, pilots
must have forty hours of
instrument flying time.
They must pass a written
test and a flying-by-
instrument test.

instruments

A pilot makes out a flight plan.

flight
instructor

flight school

Pilots who teach others to fly are called flight instructors. They are teachers in flight schools. Many flight schools are in city airports.

Connie Engla, a pilot in the United States Air Force, was the first woman to break the sound barrier. That means she flew more than seven hundred miles per hour.

Test pilots check out new airplanes. Before a buyer gets a new airplane, the test pilot flies it. The test pilot checks every part of the plane for safety.

companies

Some pilots fly for large companies. The company pilots are ready to fly company workers anywhere their business takes them. They fly the small planes and large planes owned by the company.

Many businesses have their own planes and pilots.

Both planes and helicopters are used for crop dusting.

Agricultural pilots, or ag pilots, work with farmers. They seed and fertilize fields. Sometimes they spray crops for insects. They fly low over the ground. Ag pilots are sometimes called crop dusters. Crop duster pilots do dangerous and important jobs.

crop duster

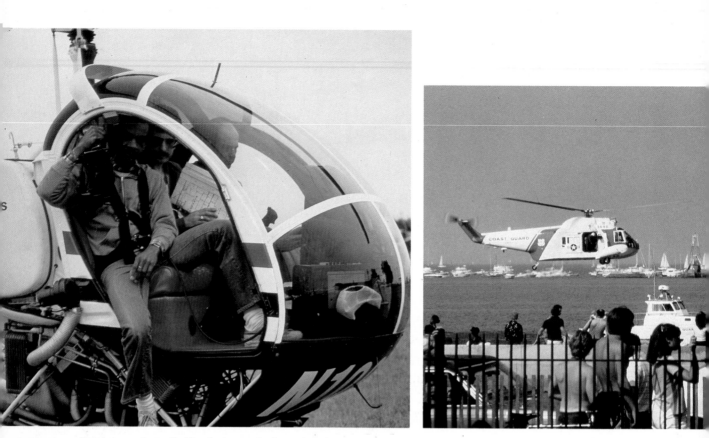

Photographers (left) often use helicopters to shoot pictures. Coast guard helicopters (right) look for boats and ships that might be in trouble.

Helicopter pilots do many jobs. They fly the aircraft "workhorses."

Helicopter pilots might be police officers or reporters.

Helicopters rush people to hospitals.

Sometimes the helicopter
is a flying ambulance.
The helicopter might be
a sky bus, moving
people from airports to
parts of a city.

flight engineer

physical exam

Pilots who work for airline companies must be college graduates. They must have flown jet airplanes. They need a commercial pilot's license and a flight engineer's license. They must be in excellent health, and pass a physical exam.

Flight simulators are machines used to check a pilot's ability
to handle emergency situations and to check on their flying
skills. Although these machines never leave the ground, they
respond to the controls the same way a plane in flight would.

Captain Paul Warf (left) and Captain Barbara Wiley (right)

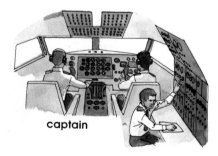

captain

The pilot in command of an airplane is the captain. Airline captains also need an airline transport pilot's license. For this license pilots must be twenty-three years old and have 1,500 hours of flying time.

A pilot checks the plane before takeoff.

Airline pilots fly jets to countries all around the world. The captain works with the copilot and the flight engineer on a large airliner.

Before takeoff, pilots check their plane. Engines and instruments

Pilots carefully plan every flight.

and all systems must be working. Pilots plan their flight. They check the weather reports. They choose how high they will fly. They choose the speed and flight path

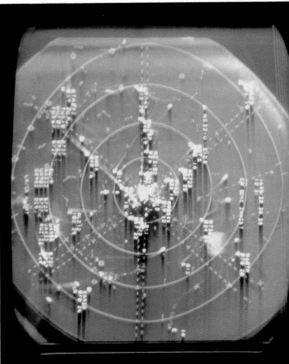

Radar (right) shows the air traffic controllers where every plane is in their air space.

they will take for the
fastest, safest flight.
Computers help them
make their plan.

flight path

air traffic control station

air traffic controllers

Air traffic control
stations help pilots along
the trip. Air traffic

Traffic controllers in the control tower (left) are in charge of all airport traffic.

controllers tell pilots when
they should change air
speed or take the airplane
higher or lower. They
let pilots know about
other airplanes nearby.

A pilot's log is a record of his trip.

When pilots land, they fill out a record of the trip, called a log.

log

Airline pilots usually fly eighty-five hours a month. This is a safety rule for the airline pilot and the passengers.

Pilot (left) makes a final check before takeoff. A pilot and copilot (right) are needed to fly this Boeing 747 jumbo jet.

Now you know about pilots. They learn to fly many different kinds of planes. Some are flight instructors or test pilots. Some fly helicopters or

crop dusters. Some carry
people and cargo in
airliners.

What kind of pilot
would you like to be?

WORDS YOU SHOULD KNOW

agricultural (ag • rih • KULCH • er • ul)—having to do with farming, or agriculture

air traffic control (AIR TRAF • ik cun • TROL)—stations that guide pilots in taking off, flying, and landing

altitude (AL • tuh • tood)—how high above the ground something is

ambulance (AM • byuh • luntz)—a vehicle for taking sick or hurt persons to a hospital

captain (KAP • tun)—the pilot in charge of an airliner

cargo (KAR • go)—things that are carried or moved in an airplane, ship, railroad, truck, etc.

copilot (KO • pie • lut)—a helper to the captain of a plane

crop duster (KRAHP DUHS • ter)—an agricultural pilot, who flies low over a field to seed, fertilize, or spray it

flight engineer (FLITE en • juh • NEAR)—a member of the crew of a large airliner who is in charge of mechanical things on the plane

flight path (FLITE PATH)—the line an airplane travels when it is in the air

helicopter (HEL • uh • kop • ter)—an airplane that has rotors, which allow it to fly up and down as well as forward

instruments (IN • struh • ments)—all the electrical and mechanical things used to make an airplane fly

license (LIES • ents)—an official paper that allows someone to do something, such as drive a car or fly a plane

log (LOG)—a record of an airplane trip, made out by the pilot

military service (MIL • uh • tair • ee SIR • vus)—the army, navy, marines, etc.

passengers (PASS • en • jers)—people who travel in an airplane, ship, train, bus

INDEX

PHOTO CREDITS

ABOUT THE AUTHOR

June Behrens has written more than fifty books, plays, and filmstrips for young people, touching on all subject areas of the school curriculum. Mrs. Behrens has for many years been an educator in one of California's largest public school systems. She is a graduate of the University of California at Santa Barbara and has a Master's degree from the University of Southern California. Mrs. Behrens is listed in *Who's Who of American Women*. She is a recipient of the Distinguished Alumni Award from the University of California for her contributions in the field of education. She and her husband live in Rancho Palos Verdes, a Southern California suburb.